Evensong

EVENSONG

Poems by Kenneth Steven

821.91
STE

First published in Great Britain in 2011

Society for Promoting Christian Knowledge
36 Causton Street
London SW1P 4ST
www.spckpublishing.co.uk

British Library Cataloguing-in-Publication Data
A catalogue record for this book is available from the British Library

ISBN 978-0-281-06480-9
eBook ISBN 978-0-281-06653-7

Typeset by Caroline Waldron, Wirral, Cheshire
First printed in Great Britain by Ashford Colour Press
Subsequently digitally printed in Great Britain

Produced on paper from sustainable forests

*This collection of poems is
for Jack Hutcheson*

Contents

Acknowledgements

Poems from *Evensong* have appeared in the following literary journals: *The Countryman, Northwords Now, The Interpreter's House, Southlight, Scintilla, Acumen, Life and Work, Epoch, Poetry Scotland, New Writing Dundee, The Fireside Book* and *Staple*. A good number of the poems have also appeared in an anthology published by the NHS in Scotland, a volume entitled *Reflections of Life*.

# A BASKET OF WATER

The boy came back from school in tatters –
A March day; snow thin in all the hills,
A blue wind breezing the sun
Wild across hillsides, and sweeping it away.
The boy saw nothing; he had told a lie –
The teacher had belted his hands until they bled.
I want to be good, he told his grandfather,
But it never lasts. I always have to start again.
The old man ruffled his hair. *Take the coal basket,*
Go down to the river and fill it –
But hurry, run for all you're worth.
The boy went, the basket bumping the backs of his legs,
Fled down the hill, wind grazing his face –
Plunged the basket deep, swirled sky water upwards,
Rushed with it splaying, up and up the hill,
So it gushed and splashed, hopeless.
He came back with an emptiness that shone –
The words in his eyes spoke dark.
The old man knelt beside him:
It wasn't useless. Look at the inside of the basket;
The coal dust's gone, it's washed away.
Just the same with you. Put good things
Deep in the heart. They'll bleed away,
But the light they give is always left behind.

 THE LINN

On August days when thunder
Prowled about the hills like bears
And skies were low and heavy
We went to swim in the river. By then
It was thin and slippery, resting in rocks,
Half-hidden under green overhangs.
But the pool was a whole stillness of smoky quartz,
Deep as a dungeon.
We skinned ourselves, crashed into the water –
Its delicious gasp of cool – plunged under
To lie on our backs breathless, listening
To the whizz of swifts above us,
The river's silvering below.
By nightfall we trailed back home, barefoot,
Smelling the blue smoke of barbecues,
Hearing in the trees muffled smudges of talk
As rain pattered dark around us
And lightning flickered the sky.

 # EASTER

When the year is beginning again,
The sleet coming in wet cotton on the wind
To build against the dykes;
And sometimes the sun like a single eye
Blind behind the clouds;
And daffodils, the frail green of them,
Hidden away and hurting in the wind –
I am no longer full of my own emptiness
But just light and sky, listening,
And able to hear at last.

 ONCE UPON A TIME

The house asleep like a blue ship under deep water;
The moon fiercing the skylight window,
I padded down, bare feet trying not to creak the stairs,
Out under the jewellery of the stars.

The hushed bark of a dog,
The last pears fallen from the tree in red-gold slush,
The moon cast over the garden, such a bright shadow
I could have wandered miles and miles.

And that was what I longed for –
To lose myself in the story of the forest,
Come out in some magical tale
Written by wolves and snow.

# MORNING

A soundless day in December;
Six below and the trees furred with frost,
The ground a snow that was not snow,
A crystalling of cold.

I went up into the Narnia of the woods,
Making my steps soft, yearning deer and geese.
I heard nothing but my own heart;
Just a shimmering of birds from one tree –
Thirty or forty in a flight that was made of waves.

There among the trees the loch;
A breath of ice had ghosted it,
An ice swivelled with patterns,
As though in the night strange dancers
Had come to skate its stillness.

I stood, scarves of breath woolling the air
As a cloth bell somewhere
Remembered Sunday.

 ALL I KNOW

The late sun leaving in the trees an orange-red,
A soft honey fire. There has been no breath of wind
In fifteen days; leaves hang gold and gorgeous
In the woods, and through them the deer tread
Patched with light, wary. The year begins to die;
The rowans hang in blood-red clutches, every day
The ripe sun is lower in the sky. Is this what it must be?
Or did everything begin to live for ever
Before the bite of the apple and the long fall
Into our own demise? Is the worm at the earth's heart
Our fault, the birth of our badness,
Or is the last blizzard of all things,
The withering of all that is, no more
Than it should be, like a child's blown bubble –
Beautiful to begin with, spinning reds and blues –
Until it fades in a ball of cobwebs, bursts
In a thistledown of drops?
All I know is the seed sleeps December long –
Forgotten, gone, buried in the dark –
And then is born again.

# MAKE-BELIEVE

There is no God nowadays,
We have grown up and gone away from home.
There is no last prayer before the light goes out –
We lie awake and wonder, and the dark is sore.

Sometimes, in the flicker of the dawn,
When the garden blooms with a thatch of birdsong –
We feel the place that joys and hurts
Empty and wanting.

Sometimes, in the suburban sadness of the last train
    going home –
Acres and acres of living rooms,
Flickering thin November rain –
We wish and know it's all too late.

We must understand the murders of children alone now;
We must put back on an old shelf the donkey and stable
We made out of wood a long time ago –
We have to believe we were wrong.

We need to keep on going
And everything will be just fine.
Of course it will – it's only a question of time,
Nothing more than a question of time.

 NOVEMBER

In winter we go whole days without seeing light –
The trees condemned, heads bowed and bare.

Except for the odd pale yellow window,
Sky and hills and woods are one, grey and dead.

Hard to believe there will be daffodils,
That green things will happen again.

At night houses shine out in cries across fields of floodwater,
The cold of wet and wind like the cut of a spade
   in a bare hand.

We pull our hopes and dreams behind us on sledges
Into the sheer hope of light,
The one clenched promise of the spring.

 SOLACE

I look back through my mind and see
The days when forest wolved the land in mystery
And light was cradled out of coracles
In wild and wintered island storm.

All night and every night the rip and snarl of wind,
And this their task alone, to guard the light they
     had been given –
The flutter of that single flame
Keeping out the whole world of the dark.

# SWALLOWS

On a day that is almost September,
Torn between sun and wind,
Like ice skaters curling the sky
They loop and skirt and lift –
Little miracles made of air.

They nest in the eaves of our porch;
Sometimes at night I open the door to the dark
To catch their jostle in the tiny light.

All these weeks and we don't even know
Their number. The young ones find the sky
As easy as breathing; catch and swivel
In a dance the same since the beginning.

Then, as though some voice has summoned them,
The swallows gather:
Africa restless deep inside,
Thousands of miles in their wings.

The following day they're gone, all of them –
And we watch where they were, wondering.

 GLIESE 581

If we should find some other star –
Half a century away, still in the silence of the sky –

We'd leave (the ones who had the money for the fare),
This planet gassed and poisoned by our wars.

We'd look back one last time in wonder
On the blue beauty of our home left empty:

A gust of toppled promises,
Growing further off (but never less).

Then dark and doubt, and fifty years
To get to somewhere only telescopes had seen;

Unbegun and perfect,
Our chance to start again.

And in the beginning we'd believe we could;
We'd keep our promises for sure.

But then the shadow of ourselves
Would fall, we would forget –

And on the eighth day
We'd be whispering for war.

 DAFFODIL

The jagged lightning that struck him once
Has left him in a wheelchair and a home.

A Sunday afternoon in April and distant relatives
Wheel him round a garden talking vaguely

Of holidays and how their son in Portugal
Is getting on with language classes.

But Paul is bundling with his hands,
Starts struggling feet that are the wrong way round:

His hands are sore and without vowels,
The big head begins to arch away in dribbles –

And they call a nurse, afraid they call a nurse.
But all he's trying to say is this.

 # SAM

The boy wanders the farm tracks
Summer and winter, going nowhere.

Who knows who his father was
(Though once upon a time they wondered).

His mother sits in the village
A law unto herself;

Secrets in her sealed lips –
Scours doorsteps twice a week

For five pounds fifty,
Her face and hands gone hard.

The boy is twenty-four;
Long ago the village teacher let him off

To wander the fields of his own thoughts
(Music and maths ran through his hands like water).

Now on windy days he goes
To Whin Top and the horse;

He wanders the long ridge
When the sky is inky and blotched,

He strokes the horse
With words in his own language,

Softens the long face,
Looks into the dun-coloured eyes –

And the horse tosses and paws
In to him, rubs that chestnut head against him.

The boy stays until the dark blue skies
Are calming, and stars splinter the night,

Then goes back gentle and himself
Home, healed.

 BELIEVING

Winter and the geese circle the fields in hunching skeins,
Everything asleep and buried, secret,
Waiting for some silent voice to waken them once more.

There among the trees, low above the ground,
The sun struggles to break through,
Pale as a daffodil, frail and failing.

To keep believing is not easy, even in December
With the child's clutter of star and donkey, gift and manger.
The dark comes back, the long dark

Searching lost through the fields. The night
Starless and empty, just rivers full of gibberish,
The morning hopeless, a grey sky low over a grey earth.

So was it just a story written long ago
Lost in the telling? Yet why then did they carry it
With such fire, dying to lions and the torment

Of wheels and spikes? Why if all of it
Was nothing more than stories?
Will not Christ return?

Two thousand years have come and gone
Yet will it happen on some late November night,
A light among the trees when all the fields are flooded;

Something to go and seek and find
Alone, that happens just to those
Who leave everything they have behind?

 CURLEWS

On windless white-blue summer nights
They swim the skies invisible,
Water voices trailing over fields
And people open wide back doors
So lemon light inside spills out.
They stand, look up and listen
Beside the fields and soft talking of the river,
As all the anger and the sadness of the world
Is gone a while, a timeless time,
Till slow and beautiful that song
Is all there is, and all there ever was.

THE SUMMER HOUSE

There is the hush of sea in an open window
And a child coming running under bare sunlight
With news of shells and a big whale.

There is more time; life slows to a single heartbeat,
The days flow into endless places, stretch like shadows.

The world we carry does not weigh so much;
But seems to fall as simple as a starfish
In something we can see is beautiful again.

Sometimes we ride the sea, go out to climb the waves,
To have the laughter knocked from us in play
And come back breathless to a barefoot house
To listen, listen to the late day made of curlews.

A huge moon rolls into the sky, ghost-white,
Lighting every field, and breeze silks the hills.

All night we dream of nothing
Like children who have never learned of sin.

 # THE DISAPPEARED

Jorge Antonio Careli
I do not know you;
Only an imprint of a name on paper
As slight as a butterfly's passing.

In the metal blue heat of Rio
In the middle of summer
You disappeared with the police
And never came back.

As it was in Russia
As it was in Germany
The little people and the grey
Taken away into nowhere.

Jorge Antonio Careli
Underground in the forgotten rooms
Of the dark and the disappeared
This is the candle I give you:

The anger of words that may light
One mind here, one there
Over and over till fires
Have burned through the locks and the chains

Until there are no more disappeared
No more detained without trial
Until there are no more naked and cold
In the horror of man's invention.

 THAW

Seven weeks of frost. A fist gripped
The fields and woods in thick ice.
The lochs were the eyes of dead fish,
White and pale and glazed. Each night
I thudded out new logs; we lit a fire
That dragoned in the hearth. Around us
In vast skies the stars glittered
And another settling of flakes
Ghosted the trees each morning.

Seven weeks of white, until today,
And a wild wind riding the hills;
Green so green the eyes cannot believe.
All of the winter gone, slid into the streams
That babble and chatter with the joy of thaw.

How little we know of the strings that hold us
Intricate in space and time.

OCTOBER

She knows that something's different
In the skies, blue but sharper than before.
The night has left the hands of leaves
Imprinted in the grass, blood-red and orange,
And there is something missing in the skies
She knows so well she cannot see.
They are not there, the swallows –
All summer they criss-crossed her day
Their tassels swimming the water of the air
Through all the still blue nights that would not die,
Which kept blue-gold and visible till midnight,
The swallows always there, celebrating and trapezing,
Missing not a single catch.

But yesterday they were ready:
Their journey restless in them – flitting,
Jostling and whispering along the wires –
The whole way back to Africa
Mapped minutely in those wings.
She watched them then, yet had not thought
That night would blow them all away.

What will the winter be without them?
Lanes like the beds of rivers, gullied deep with leaves
And the trees masts, leaning out of huge winds
To whelm the valleys. The black horse of night
Galloping through earlier and earlier, leaving things huge –
The lit eyes of houses staring afraid,
Like silent cries for help.

Yet they will come back, as all things that we fear are gone,
Return, somehow. Just as the new horns of buds
Will green the trees, and ripened fields of sun
Will rise to life – the swallows will be there again.
She will see them when she least expects to,
Will find them in that late blue light
Just as she always has.

 ONE WINTER

We went to the woods for holly
On days that were five below;
The river a glass slide, the skies such pale blue
The world was a kind of white.

Waxy snippets for Christmas
With berries robin bright;
Bags of rustling handfuls,
No heavier than thin air.

We came back from the glades with hands
All red and raw, words slurred.
Somewhere a muffled snowball sun;
In the trees only crows and quiet.

We came back and crackled holly
Into every corner we could;
Lit a fire that thundered the chimney,
Crouched in its glare till we glowed.

 HARVEST

Old ways are no more; most men are redundant,
Empty-handed, grandsons of farm labourers
Gone from the land, who do not know the difference
Between lathes and spades. Once in a while perhaps,
They stop beside a road and see
The white kite of the moon being hoisted
Into a huge pale sky; for the first time they listen
To the wind ripple silver through the fields.
Something of all the autumns there have ever been
Remembers them, kindles a place
Lost and long forgotten.

 # SIGNING

On a train eager with June children,
The level heat dizzy in the fields –
I saw two women leaning in together,
Intent, talking in total silence.

Their hands moved like rabbits in a moonlit field –
Flitting, making shapes, fleetingly,
Out of fingers that were never still,
Except to listen to the answer that came back
Drawn out of empty air.

I watched them hungrily, eavesdropping,
On a conversation I could never hear.

 DOVES

Talking with the man on the bus
From Iona to the end of Mull
And thinking of his white papers for defence
That had fluttered like doves from Whitehall
I still told him where the otters were
And the relics of the Gaelic poets
Thinking how small he would be
Playing God with a chessboard of figures
Bombs at his disposal
In some lonely corridor of power
Where something as lovely as a sunset
Or the crying of a curlew
Would never come.

 WILD IRISES

A gale of children swept in today
With wild bunches of flowers.
They left them laughing on the kitchen table
And in a gust were gone.

All day they ran themselves free
Up hills and down;
At seven they came home, blown out,
Sunset burning their faces.

Now the house is fast asleep;
It leans into the wind, smoke
Hurrying at an angle from the chimney –
The flowers on the table shining.

BEHIND THE WHITE

When I was seventeen
I worked as a cleaner
In the hospital next door.

Everything was white: the walls,
The floors, the uniforms, the talk.
Everyone whispered in white.

And every day I cleaned the room
Of a woman who could not walk or talk,
Who could not move or eat.

She lay in her own room
And a single plastic pipe
Attached her to a huge machine.

All she could move were her eyes.
I polished the floor around her, and her eyes
Came after me.

I was so afraid of the darkness I saw there
I thought if I looked too long
I'd fall in and drown.

Thirty years she'd been there;
Left in that bed like something
Washed up from a storm, like a bird with broken wings.

And sometimes I lay in the dark at home, dreamless,
And wondered if she hadn't passed the place
Where once she was meant to die.

 # FOG

Trees that last night
Were statements, exclamation marks

Have lost their nerve. The river
Is not sure where to go.

There is a silence not easy to breathe;
The air is damaged, fills the lungs like candyfloss.

Sheep come out of nowhere
Surprised by their own appearance,

Noising blares of questions.
Only a wren lets out trinkets of song

Like a liquid silver, somewhere among
What once were bushes.

A train burns north, a curl of glow-worm
Burrowing into the white nothingness of the distance.

 FOR JOHN CLARE

Come then, trust my hand and let me take you
Out into the sunlight. See how the clouds part
And April blesses everything again.

Remember how feet felt slippered by the moss,
A wren sputtering bright trinkets of song,
And in among the trees a stream talking to itself.

Look, a badger! Over there,
Snouting the ground with his striped head;
Your smile remembers, and the softness of your eyes.

You don't need the voices any more;
You've listened to their insane babble long enough –
It's all right now, it's over. I'll take you home.

 THE CARPENTER

for three years he did nothing but work with wood;
he'd served his apprenticeship, root and branch,
could smooth the roughness from damaged goods
and cut to the living heart

the sap that ran him was pure
flowed through hands and words
a whole song, so they marvelled
at something they'd never heard

except he was just too good:
in the end they took his own tools,
killed him on a hill
with wood and nails

three days he lay
a seed in the sleeping earth, until
he burst open, back and beautiful –
here, and here, and here, and here

 A POEM

Sometimes it is no more extraordinary
Than going for water from a well.

Or a bird coming soft as a cloth out of winter sky
To alight on the palm of your hand.

 LENIN

When he was eight on his father's farm
They drove back one night with the sledge
Through huge darkness. And then a fox
Dying in the snow, blood dripping like time
From a broken jaw. He cradled the injured thing
The whole way home, only its red shadow
Left against his chest when they went inside at last.

A whole five days he mourned that fox
And still could not forget. Then it was as if
He woke from some deep slumber, a change
Glittering his eyes. He went outside to cut wood
With the new axe, slice after slice after slice.

 SHALLOWATER

The river was furry with insects;
the moon caught in the trees
like a silver fish, glittering and magical.
The swallows flicking the air,
weaving the still night in darts,
their wings no louder than breaths.

And I thought what it might be like
if you were with me
this midnight at midsummer;
how we'd whisper the grass to the river
to swim naked in soft swivels
in the warm blue moonlight.

Thinking aloud a whole new land –
ideas and dreams and longings –
a language strange to our tongues,
its syllables and vowels
around us like strange fire:
make-believe beginning to be.

 ROMJULA

Between Christmas and New Year
The days are nameless; they lie lost and strange.

Mist drifts the wood and river in thin scarves;
The cold is raw and sore.

Geese drift the skies in straggled arrowheads,
Splay down in broken fragments through the slush.

I go for walks and don't know where to go;
I come back home and thud out logs to burn,

That dragon in the hearth each night with orange flames,
That fire our watching eyes.

We wait and wait, patient –
Not knowing what it is we're waiting for.

 THE FISHING

The burn flowed down the hillside
Like a tousled collie. We climbed and climbed.
A spit of rain in the air; edges of sky
Furred with mist. And there, the loch, at last,
Like a gem in the brooch of the moors.

The canvas bag with the rod,
The sizzle of the reel,
The search for the best place to cast.

I chased a blue gust of damselflies
Then sat and listened to the silence;
The huge emptiness of the hills
Buried under a rubble of cloud.

There was always one fish, slippery,
And the heathery smoke of a fire,
Till the dark sank and the rain began for good.

I see it now, years back across the moorland,
That what mattered was not the fish at all
But everything else.

 TRANSCENDENCE

in those last days of war, in 1918,
the soldier poet Wilfred Owen seemed to change

there under the mess of wire, of trampled horses,
trampled men, a mire mile after long mile
to the very edges of the sky
this stark, raving madness of a landscape

it is as though one night on sentry duty
underneath the whole galleon of the moon
all lay clear for him, as men slept
those precious hours before the dawn

and somehow he was transformed
for something plated him, scaled him silver –
    radiant, flickering –
so in those last days, his own days,
he did not walk, he flew

 THE QUINCES

That autumn we stayed in an old manse;
A place full of ticking clocks that sounded
Like disapproving Victorian gentlemen.

At breakfast between a hurry of bowls and courses
She told us of the laden trees in the garden,
All those quinces she hadn't had time to pick.

Late that afternoon I went out
Under the blue-cold skies of October
A world closed in by trees and crows.

A low sun pierced the woods in a bonfire of light;
All round the house the lanes
Were gullies of red and gold leaves.

But that garden was yellow-white globes on branches
The colour of mistletoe berries, lamps of things
Shaped like pears.

Their stalks broke like ice,
Cracked in the frozen stillness –
I put them, piece by piece, in a basket.

I went back, wondering what her kitchen would smell like –
What things it would make for the winter –
The quinces frothing in pans like lava.

 AFTERWARDS

Four days they searched, the sea out of its mind.
The children went back to school
Glitter-eyed, their laughter quick and wrong.
Inside the house the radio talked to itself
Whole days, a babble of noise.
She stood on the washing green,
The morning torn between blue and grey, the clothes
Thrashing the wind, her face ploughed and small.
No one talked about it when they came to call
Because the silence of the story lay everywhere –
Open-mouthed, a frozen scream.

 SANCTUARY

After the last fires in the sky
there was nothing, just the empty humming of the wires,
the roads grey rivers stretching out of sight.

We left with no more than we could carry
as our ancestors did, back in the days before
we began to want more than ever we had needed.

All those we passed were scatter-eyed and empty;
they carried their children close like their own hunger –
we heard their stories in their silence.

We had been following a strange cloud a long time
when we descended into a deep green place,
stopped, set down our loads and stood:

A waterfall like the tail of a white horse,
a pool underneath of dark quartz,
a meadow, sheltered and full of wild flowers.

We looked and listened and we knew –
a sanctuary, held in the hands of the hills.

 THREE DAYS

I

All day under the circling
The golden hugeness of the sun
Beat by beat the maddening, terrible day
The terrible madness until, suddenly, at last
The sky went ugly with bruises, a thunder stuttered
In the red hills and the rain came hard as grapes
heavy, hissing, huge, and lightning gouged the dust.
His face, she saw his face, her son
The son she'd brought into a stable
Shining with bright rain and blood in rivers
And how his head slipped forwards, finished
His shoulders torn like wings, like angel wings
Broken now for ever by the weight
Of this last loss of God.
But even then they waited, the soldiers and the priests
Watching him with gaping mouths as if they still expected
He might speak or heal or teach.
They watched the rain shine his shoulders and his broken head
Hour after hour after hour
As if they feared him still.

II

Nothing. All through the night
Listening and locking doors, whispering
Just in case. Shadows
Ghosting the streets, the gnaw
Of hunger. The going over and over
The ashes of the days, searching
For something that might make sense.
No star in the sky, no light –
Just the wound of morning in the end,
Before remembering, before trying to pray
In the empty silence of the walls
And feeling all the words like dust
Scattered and blown away.
The slow beat of time, hour by hour
Like drops of blood, like drops of grief
Till night and sleepless dark.

III

It was over. They left Jerusalem in the dead of night;
No light alive, the grey rocks of the last days
Raw and jagged in their throats.
They were fishermen, went back, broken
To the only thing they knew, to Galilee.

And all night nothing;
The skies aubergine, a piling of bruised clouds,
The lake eerie and moonless, creeping with shadows,
The cold leaking into feet and hands like leprosy.

Dawn was a wound in the east, a gash,
The twist of a rusted knife.
And there a figure on the shore beside a fire,
Someone who seemed to wait for them.
They drudged up the boats, deep into dry sand.
He spoke to them with his eyes,
Gave them pieces of smoky fish.

They knew him when he called them by their names.

# LULLABY FOR THE DAYS
THAT LIE AHEAD

As the ridge of Norway passes
And the sea sleeps still and blue

There you lie curled far away
With a child's tight clasp of faith.

And the child inside you also
Sleeps unknown in that strange sea

Keeping hidden, deep in secret
All their days and dreams to come

Still unwritten, still unspoken
Still intact inside their shell.

Now the day is almost breaking
Now the night is almost done

And I pray for light and wonder
For this road unknown we share.

 CLEARING THE SNOW

we breasted waves of it, waist deep
to make some kind of path

spaded thick white air
for hours and hours

spooning candyfloss
that grew to castle shapes

tunnelling the silence
till we broke through at last

the wood went blue with nightfall
stars flickering the sky

we stood and looked down
on a town left powerless

not a jewellery of light
but the colour of a bruise

and I stopped and thought
how snow could bring us back

to nothing but the night
how all that separates

our ancestors from us
is electricity

 ENDPIECE

Last year in Greenland I bought it
Under great whales of mountains by a sea of ice,
From a table of things all carved from shining:
Little men threading water, their softstone canoes,
Walrus rearing at harpoons in mid-roar.

Now, all this time later, that place
Remains like some story from a book.
I turn it in the light, my polar bear on a pad of ice,
And think of the world wilting in the sun's wrath,
And nowhere left for the polar bear to go.

 ARGYLL, OCTOBER

out at the sea's edge
the whole wind riding the day
the bracken crippled and whipped
the sometimes of light blown away

here in huddles of stone
a whole millennium before us
men from Ireland made chapels
found God in these blown wide skies

further in, where boats nodded and rocked
in little creeks of sun under overhangs of oak
we listened to the psalms of blackbirds

 EVENSONG, AMPLEFORTH

I open the door and walk;
Stone booms and hisses underneath my feet.

The choirboys sing, shrill and beautiful –
A song woven of ancient words,
A Latin crossing to another land,
Its loaves and fishes, ochre light.

I do not know the words and yet I sing;
The day is done, light sinks –
My life is open to the sky.